DELIVERED
BRINGING FORTH DELIVERANCE BY THE POWER OF GOD

DR. MERCHELE ROBINSON

Copyright © 2020 by Dr. Merchele Robinson

DELIVERED

All rights reserved. No part of this publication may be reproduced, distributed, or transmitted in any form or by any means, including photocopying, recording, or other electronic or mechanical methods, without the prior written permission of the publisher, except in the case of brief quotations embodied in critical reviews and certain other noncommercial uses permitted by copyright law. For permission requests, write to the publisher, addressed "Attention: Permissions Coordinator," at info@beyondpublishing.net

Quantity sales special discounts are available on quantity purchases by corporations, associations, and others. For details, contact the publisher at the address above.

Orders by U.S. trade bookstores and wholesalers. Email info@BeyondPublishing.net

The Beyond Publishing Speakers Bureau can bring authors to your live event. For more information or to book an event contact the Beyond Publishing Speakers Bureau speak@BeyondPublishing.net

The Author can be reached directly at

Manufactured and printed in the United States of America distributed globally by BeyondPublishing.net

New York | Los Angeles | London | Sydney

ISBN: 978-1-952884-84-9

TABLE OF CONTENTS

Chapter 1: *Do You Want to Be Free?* 7

Chapter 2: *Your Deliverance is Your Decision* 11

Chapter 3: *The Oil Overflows* 15

Chapter 4: *Put on the Helmet of Salvation* 19

Chapter 5: *Your Blessings Are on Their Way* 25

Chapter 6: *Spiritual Blessings Come First* 29

Chapter 7: *Let God Let His Light In* 35

Chapter 8: *Salvation—the Ultimate Deliverance* 39

Chapter 9: *God Delivers Us from Evil and Darkness* 43

Chapter 10: *A Miracle for You* 47

Chapter 11: *Giving Back to the Lord* 51

CHAPTER 1

DO YOU WANT TO BE FREE?

You can be delivered!

There is healing for a hurting heart.

When you feel pain, it's hard to see the light, or see how the experience fits into the bigger picture of things. You become overtaken by the trauma and even the drama associated with your experiences.

At a very young age, God taught me that the struggles in our lives are opportunities for us to be healed and made whole. Like so many young women, I found myself looking for love in all the wrong places.

Life Guarantees Disappointments

Understand this: whenever we stray away from our upbringing and our parents' advice, the devil has traps waiting for us. I say that because I ended up in a relationship that took my life into a direction that I never imagined going in.

I believe that everyone makes mistakes, and often, it is not the mistakes that define a person's character, but what they do afterward. I hoped in my heart that this man would redeem himself, be accountable for his actions, and work for my forgiveness. I hung on to the faith that he would step up to be the man I thought he was. But he didn't. And I found myself needing to be healed, instead.

Like so many reading this book, my pain was prophetic, because it was my pain that led me to God. There I was, broken-hearted and in need of healing, roughly in the year of 1987. I found myself in Now Faith Church of God in Christ, and Pastor Dorothy Nelson was engaged in a powerful revival where souls were being saved, healed, set free, and delivered. And this is why I say, when you are in need of deliverance and healing, you need more than a religious experience— you need to be up under an anointing that can destroy the yokes of the enemy assigned to your life.

Evangelist Dorothy Nelson would teach and preach until deliverance would break out all over the church. The prophetic would be so strong and so powerful that the only reason a person would stay bound was if they didn't really want to be free.

I wanted to be free!

I wanted to be delivered!

I wanted to be healed!

So, I placed a demand on God every time I went to church, and I believe God saw my sincerity, and He set me free. I have never turned back ever since!

No Drive-By Deliverances

Listen, I believe that I am anointed to release healing and deliverance into your life. You might be reading this book in need of a healing or deliverance and I'm led now to declare over your life that you can be delivered! If God could heal my heart and deliver me from the destruction of the enemy, then I declare He will do the same thing for you!

Now this can't be a drive-by deliverance. I say that because so many come to church simply to be delivered, and after they get their deliverance, you don't see them until they need another one. But when I came to Jesus, I was delivered and *I committed to Him as well!*

I stayed up under the anointing until the Word got in me. I declare even now that, like me, your pain is creating a path to power! You are about to experience the supernatural power of God. It will overtake you like never before, and your life will never be the same again!

Now when God brings healing and deliverance to your life, make sure you stay where God plants you. Don't allow the enemy to uproot you. Be steadfast, unmoved, always abounding in the work of the Lord, for your labor shall not be in vain.

Allow me to pray over your life…

> *I decree and declare that the power of an almighty God bless you right now and that a birthing of healing and deliverance like never before happens. I pray that the powers of darkness are released from your life forever and that you walk in total victory in Jesus' name! Amen!*

CHAPTER 2

YOUR DELIVERANCE IS YOUR DECISION

Don't give the Devil any mercy!

Listen. This is the chapter where I need your undivided attention. You cannot afford to multitask while reading this chapter. God has assigned me to you to get you ready to experience an impartation that will change your entire life!

Don't Give Satan the Edge

While in prayer, the Lord began to deal with me concerning how the people of God have allowed the enemy to rule and run them over. The Lord began to show me that when we give in to the schemes of the enemy, we empower him to get the victory over us.

2 Corinthians 2:11 says, "Lest Satan should get an advantage of us, for we are not ignorant of his devices."

What this passage is saying is simply this: if you and I are ignorant of Satan's devices, our ignorance gives him the advantage. This is why so many believers are losing the war against the enemy, because they are assisting him by giving him the advantage.

You have got to know how the enemy operates, so that when he launches an attack against you, you won't be caught off guard. Also, you have got to know the systems of Satan. If he cannot defeat you, he will attack your marriage, children, physical body, business, job, mind, finances, and he will even attack your spirit.

Power Over the Devil

I'm anointed to tell you that you have power over the Devil! Did you hear what I just said? You have power over the Devil and the works of darkness. The very moment this hit your spirit, you take back the advantage you gave to the enemy.

Luke 10:19 says, "Behold: I give unto you power to tread on serpents and scorpions, and over all the power of the enemy, and nothing shall by any means hurt you."

This is what the Devil doesn't want you to know—that God has given you power over the enemy—but you have got to make up your mind to use the power He gave you. God equips those He calls, and He calls those He equips.

You have to take authority over the enemy— every dark place, every wicked spirit, and all of the evil activity sent your way by the enemy. Here's something I discovered when I was being delivered: it is that if the enemy can't deceive you himself, he will work through those who have access to you.

I will never forget when I was involved with someone whom I sincerely loved. I mean, I was blinded by the love I had for this man. We both were a part of the same ministry at the time. And it was not until I got delivered that I was able to see how the enemy was using him to pull me out of the will of God.

We would fuse and fight about me tithing or giving sacrificially after every service. And these are things that are allowing me to walk in blessings and overflow, even now. Most nights, after a powerful worship experience, I would go home, and we would go at each other like cats and dogs, because the enemy didn't want me to believe in what I was being taught, and the enemy certainly didn't want me to practice what I was being taught. To this day, I still recognize this enemy at work in the lives of those I encounter.

You see, I'm operating in the manifestation of the Word now, but while I always had the gift, I didn't always practice using it. I remember being about 24 years old, and a team of psychics came to me and offered me to relocate to join them because of this gift. I now know that this was the Devil working behind the scenes, so that I wouldn't walk into my prophetic purpose. If you make the step, God will send the help!

Deliverance Through the Body of Christ

One night, when I was watching Christian television, Dr. Oral Roberts— who has now gone home to be with Lord— ministered to me in such a powerful way. That evening, I made up my mind to not live another day like I was living then. The moment I decided to cut the cord and walk away, God started sending people into my life to get me to a place of deliverance and to train me to deliver others.

I will never forget how Evangelist Dorothy Nelson, Apostle Lloyd Benson, Bishop G.A. Spears, and Pastor Lester Richard, Sr. all helped to get me delivered. They prepared me to identify those who needed to be delivered and to usher them to their place of deliverance.

Whenever a person walked into my presence, I could read them like a book, whether I wanted to or not. This is a gift God has given me. If you're going to get your deliverance, you must stop giving the Devil mercy, and you must send him back to the pit from whence he came.

Had I allowed the Devil to hinder me, I would not be in the place I am today. Your deliverance is *your* decision. I command you to take your rightful place and know that you have power over the enemy. I release my faith, even now over your life, so that you will receive not just supernatural power, but supernatural insight, so that you can take back the advantage you have given to the enemy and walk into complete deliverance in Jesus' name. Amen!

CHAPTER 3

THE OIL OVERFLOWS

Once you let go, the *Oil flows*—the Spirit of God flows. When you have a gift that God has given you, you get joy and happiness from above. When God anoints me and gifts me with the fresh Oil, the Oil shows up, and it flows with liberty.

Luke 4:18 (NIV) says, "The Spirit of the Lord is on me, because He has anointed me (with the oil) to proclaim good news to the poor. He has sent me to proclaim freedom for the prisoners and recovery of sight for the blind, to set the oppressed free."

Make up your mind today. I urge you to claim your deliverance: receive the anointing of God's Oil, and wait no longer.

Who or What Do You Love More?

I had to be delivered, and I didn't want to pay the price to be set free. But quitting was not an option for me. I wanted to be delivered, but I didn't want to go through the pain and the hell. I wanted to be delivered, but I didn't want the embarrassment that came with it. I refused to come out of my toxic relationship. I felt great shame, and my pride was bruised. But I still held onto my shame and pride, more than wanting to be delivered!

This reminded me of Romans 12:2-3. "And do not be conformed of this world, but be transformed by the renewing of your mind that you may prove what is that good and acceptable and the perfect will of God." So, I made up my mind to be delivered and to let go of my embarrassment, pride, and shame so I could be anointed by God.

Through this process, I realized I loved my man more than I did God. I loved my friends more than I did God. People were my problem, and I had to make up my mind to let them go. It was time to let go, to stop lying to myself, and to be set free.

The Anointing of the Oil Overflows

During services at church, God shows me a sign when the service is about to shift gears. Even before I step into the church, I arrive in my church parking lot and start feeling something in the palm of my hand. When inside the church, I start to sense His Light shining in my office, and when I come out of my office, this Oil starts dripping in my hand, in the pulpit, and I immediately start flowing in the service.

The Scripture says to lay hands on the sick. The Oil of God's Spirit messes with the Devil's plans. It shows up in the services, and people start getting delivered from drugs, gambling, and stealing. He fixes their situations, not only because they wanted it to be fixed, but it was just their time to be delivered.

Satan knows that God's people who have faith will destroy everything that he has plotted to do. The Word says that Satan comes to steal, kill, and destroy, but God says He came so that we would have life. The Scripture says the anointing can dismantle the yoke upon us.

Even when you're in the toughest of times, this is when God's Oil can show up the greatest. Psalm 23:5 (NIV) says, "You prepare a table before me in the presence of my enemies. You anoint my head with oil; my cup overflows." Can you picture this? God anoints your head with His Oil, even with your enemies surrounding you. Hallelujah! Glory to God!

God anointed me so that I would use this gift for His glory, and I don't take it for granted. People of God: His Oil is in my hand, and your faith has increased through His Word. The Word says to let the weak say, "I am strong". Whenever deliverance needs to take place and the Oil of God is dripping, I simply lay hands on the individual for deliverance in Jesus' name.

CHAPTER 4

PUT ON THE HELMET OF SALVATION

I want to talk about Bible-sphere and about the power of the thoughts in your mind. Your mind has to be protected. That is why the Apostle Paul told us to "put on the helmet of salvation". Because the attack is against our lives, we got to put the helmet on because of the mental attacks. That means it is the mind that the enemy is attacking. When you read Psalm 119, it says, "You have laid down precepts that are to be fully obeyed," which means you got to fix your mind. It is our minds that we have got to furnish with the Word of God.

The Helmet is the Word

You got to furnish your mind just like when you're in a place that is empty, you have to fill it up. It means that when your mind gets attacked, it won't do us any good to have it empty of the Word of God. He said that the Word shall return back void—Glory to God. No matter what the hell you're going through, no matter how you're challenged, we will not be defeated if we are in the Word of God. The Word of God says, "Let these minds of ours be in Christ Jesus," because it is a place of peace. Your mind can be fulfilled in the Word of Light—Glory to God! The Word will give you life, and the Word will give you more in abundance than what you ask for.

The Bible says that a double-minded man is unstable. We've got to be stable in these last days, because the enemy that is constantly attacking our mind and the relationships we're in. Many relationships do not last because we are weak when the men attack women's minds, the women attack men's minds. So, again, we must put the helmet on. We must stay in God's Word. When you put the helmet on and keep yourself in God's Word, God is protecting you.

Whenever you play football, and you've got a son who plays football, what do they do? They put their helmets on. Why do they put their helmets on? It's because they don't want to get fractures or concussions, since it is guaranteed they will get hit. Tell somebody, Glory to God! I must put my helmet on, and you must, too. Would you ever trust a coach who lets a player go out on the football field without a helmet?

Am I talking to anybody here? In other words, I feel the Holy Ghost and what I feel in my spirit is, if you're in the Word of God, then, you can guide your mind. You can let this mind of yours be in Christ, and then you won't have to wrestle with whatever the hell you're going through or the onslaught on your mind. Remember, the enemy is not going to aim for your heart first, because you're in love with God. But it's our minds we got to guide to overcome the enemy's assault.

I'm going to go to Ephesians 6 and 7, where it says to put on salvation as your helmet and to meditate on the words of the Spirit. That's right, you've got to track each spirit by the Holy Spirit and see if it's of God. You've got to check people out, and you got to see if they are of God, and when we don't, we all become hurt and attacked. I'll remind you again—the enemy will come to steal, to kill, and to destroy—but the Word of God says that, what? *You may have life*! Tell somebody, "I'm getting life this time, because I'm in the Word, down low, on the inside of me. When we have our helmet of salvation on, we got the Word of God to keep us stable and strong.

Glory to God! The Bible says that we are more than conquerors in Christ Jesus. The Word says there is nothing that will be able to separate you from the love of God that is in Christ Jesus, because what you get from God, you can keep forever, since it is everlasting. Why? Because *He* is the everlasting God—yes, He is! You must know that you've got a helmet on your head, so no matter what you're going through, the undying love of God is *for* you. And this love and His Word will protect you. Glory be to God—somebody needs to say "protect your mind!"

The Helmet is Protection

When you don't protect your mind, people will turn you down. They will make you feel real small, and you may start thinking that you're more than what you are, but guess what? With the Word of God in you, you will know humility and victory. You will be more than a conqueror that is in Christ Jesus. Let people say what they want to say, but what we know that what we do for Christ is going to last.

Believe that what you sow to God is going to prosper and so, be careful around negative people. Come on and put a helmet on! The helmet will only protect you, since the helmet is the love and Word of God! What did Isaiah say? "No weapon formed against you and your family shall prosper."

I come to tell you all that God has said, that He is coming to promote you all into this new space, like He did for Joseph. Do not be intimidated.

Stand in the Lord, and your mind will be your garrison. You will do what God says you can do. You will go wherever God says you can go.

Glory be to God! Whatever God says I can possess is already mine, and it's already yours. In other words, you've got to put this helmet on—it is your protection. Is this drilled into your head and heart yet? When it comes down to your wife, and when it comes down to your husband, we've all got to put a helmet on. Relationships can be tough, but what do you do? I'm all about the rewind, and I say when you're going through hell, can you think straight? When you're going through hell, can you pray, knowing that you are protected by the Lord?

Let me go to Ephesians 1 and 3, and, then, I'm about to do an 180 on y'all. Ephesians 1 and 3 is written to *dear brothers and sisters*. God is talking to y'all tonight! He says if another believer is overcome by sinners, then those who are godly should gently and humbly help that person back on the right path. Oh my, that means that God says we got to help them, and be careful not to fall in the same temptation ourselves. We first got to protect ourselves and then, we can help our neighbor. Hallelujah!

God Looks at the Heart

Glory to God! How can deliverance come forth when we both got the same problem? How can the blind help the blind? When we know God is a problem solver, we are overcomers. We are more in Christ Jesus. We got to be real believers, we got to be real people of God. You can't be lip talking, you gotta come from the heart. If you're being fake, God sees through this. Because God looks straight at your heart, not at the clothes you're wearing, nor the smile on your face. God sees the true you.

Before we got married, I couldn't tell my husband, *I love you*. It had to come from my heart, and because I knew I could be in love with him today and fall out of love tomorrow, I did not say it. But when I'm rooted in the Word of God, the Devil can't bring me out of it. I can stand secure and stand firm. Nobody will move me from where I stand, and I can confidently say *I love God!*

When God was choosing a king, he chose differently than how people thought He would choose. He didn't look at what people looked at, He looked right at the heart. In I Samuel 16:7 (NIV), God said, "Do not consider his appearance or his height, for I have rejected him. The Lord does not look at the things people look at. People look at the outward appearance, but the Lord looks at the heart."

If a heart is not into a real relationship, it will fall, and it won't last. I feel the Holy Ghost here—it will not last—because what you do from your heart reaches God. What you do for Christ is going to last, and that's why the Scriptures say that what God joins together, no one—including the Devil—is able to separate it. We're going to have our ups, we're going to have our downs, and so, we need to stay rooted in the Word of God with all our hearts and minds.

Tell somebody beside you, *you've got to put your helmet on*. If you don't put your helmet on, you're going to suffer from the enemy's attacks, and he will take advantage of you. You know a player can't get fractures because he's got his helmet on. How many people pray, *God, I need you to protect me! I need you to protect me!* Don't just pray this. You must upgrade your thinking.

When Paul lifted his thoughts up, he went into deep prayer. He said he prayed over everything. Do you pray over everything? When you start praying and supplications start going up, blessings are surely going to come down. But we've got to guide our minds and keep them on track. Where is your mind today? What are you thinking about? Our God is over the universe, and *even He* will still lift us up in prayer. He's not too busy to forget about each one of us. Glory to God!

CHAPTER 5

YOUR BLESSINGS ARE ON THEIR WAY

God is present, and He will breathe life upon you. That means that if God breathes on it, He is going to show up for you. Tell somebody, *I'm about to get a miracle in my house.* Look at somebody and say, *I'm about to get a miracle in my house.* Glory to God!

Abundant Blessings from Above

When you become pregnant with this truth, God says to get ready to receive all the spiritual blessings in the heavenly places. Glory be to God—your blessings are in the heavenly places! Be courageous and be bold! When the eagle sees a storm, he never gets fearful, and you can't get fearful because you're going through hell.

2 Corinthians 9:8 (NIV) says, "And God is able to bless you abundantly, so that in all things, at all times, having all that you need, you will abound in every good work." This doesn't just say God will bless us. But God will bless you and me *abundantly*! Have you ever had abundance? God is about abundance. He is ready to give you abundance today.

You better say it now, *Glory to God!* Let me tell you something—when you keep on saying what you're about to get and eventually get ready for it to show up, God will wire blessings to you. When God gets ready to wire His blessings, nobody knows when they're going to get it. When I get ready to wire somebody some money, nobody knows that I'm getting ready to do it besides God and me. This is between you and God, and the angel who He's going to send it through.

Tell someone, *an angel is getting ready to send me my stuff*. An eagle is never fearful whenever there's a storm. You better share this with some people tonight, because they're going need this glory from God! We've got some folks who are fearful, and they don't even know if they are going to last, but I've come to tell you tonight that you don't have to worry.

God says to never worry about the storm. Don't worry about tomorrow, and don't worry about what's going on with COVID-19, because I learned that the eagle flies, and when it flies, it flies right into the skies. It's up to you to be that eagle. Be bold and brave in stormy times. God, Himself, says not to worry, because everything is in His Hands. Hallelujah!

And when the eagle gets ready to fly, sometimes, it takes a curve. The reason it takes the curve is because it's taking some pressure off of God's people who've got the helmet on. And when the pressure goes off of you, that means that the pressure of the storm is now above the storm. You might be going through some hell right now, but guess what? Give it another week or two, and that hell will be up under you. Because God said you're going to have to start thinking and flying above the storm. You and I are going to have to start thinking above our circumstances.

Guard Your Minds

So, no matter what you're going through, what you're thinking, you've got to be on top. That's the part of our mind where we got to be guided, because the Scripture says to cast down every imagination. The enemy will put things in our mind, and we've got to pull it down. Tell somebody, *you've got to pull it down.* That means that we've got to think above our circumstances. It is natural for the Devil to bring things up in our minds, and we've got to cast it down and get on top of that thing. God said He is the Alpha and the Omega. He is the Beginning and the End. And He is ready to help us guard our minds in Him.

Philippians 4:7 (NIV) says, "And the peace of God, which transcends all understanding, will guard your hearts and your minds in Christ Jesus." God's peace will guard our heart, and He'll guard our minds, too. God's peace will keep our minds at peace, even when everything around us is falling apart, or it's stagnant, and nothing's going on.

No matter what you're thinking, you've got to be on top! You've got to keep His Word in your mind and be on top. Be on top of your health condition, and walk in His truth. You've got to be on top of your financial issues, you've got to be on top of your marriage, and you've got to be on top of your unemployment.

3 John 1:2-4 (NIV) states, "Dear friend, I pray that you may enjoy good health and that all may go well with you, even as your soul is getting along well. It gave me great joy when some believers came and testified about your faithfulness to the truth, telling how you continue to walk in it. I have no greater joy than to hear that my children are walking in the truth."

You're already above it spiritually, and you've got to be in heavenly places, because when God gives us miracles, the miracles come from heaven. We got to walk in the truth, so it will go well with us. You may feel deep into your issue, but your head has got to be filled in His Truth and above the issues. Wherever you head is, the Light of God in you will follow. Hallelujah!

CHAPTER 6

SPIRITUAL BLESSINGS COME FIRST

God has already blessed us with a spiritual blessing—He already *has* blessed us. What we've got to do is start thinking above, above the things keeping us down. What does this mean? Any blessing that you get, you get in your spirit. Imagine there is a multimillionaire right here by you now, but your bank account is broke. It is in the negative, and there's a terrible debt. But in your spirit, there is a blessing from the Lord. When you think your thoughts in the heavenly places, you're going to see blessings in the spirit.

Ephesians 1:3 says, "Praise be to the God and Father of our Lord Jesus Christ, who has blessed us in the heavenly realms with every spiritual blessing in Christ.

Glory to God! When we think, we've got to think in the spirit. We can't think in the natural. You got to think about your spiritual account first, since this is what God blesses first, and that's what I'm trying to tell you all. We are serving God, a wealthy God, and we are the workforce. God is the one who has the money. He's the one that holds the money, He's the one who has got the funds, and you're the one who has got a part of the money, but you haven't got all of your money yet. So, in other words, God is saying if you want the rest of your funds, your wealth, what you've got to do first is, you've got to experience wealth in your spirit.

Christy's Story:

Here is sister Christy's story, as an example. Christy said she wanted a baby and wanted to get pregnant. And therefore, the baby's going to show up as soon as the blessing hits her spirit. Does anybody hear me? Somebody? God says He's getting ready to move back here, and He's getting ready to tap into your spirit. He's getting ready to wire some money into your bank account. That's why you can't measure whenever somebody tells you what you're worth. You're about to be, not another millionaire, but a billionaire.

I've only just got dollars, but, baby, I need millions. Maybe you've got millions, so, then, you need billions. If you're living in an apartment, you're ready for a house. If you live in a house, you better be moving into a mansion. If you're driving a Toyota, it's time to get ready to drive a new car that's bigger, better, and greater.

See, for some folks, you know you gotta go up high, and you gotta speak high up. In other words, what I'm saying is, don't look at any man for help, because of what he got on the house. Don't look at a woman just because of how she's dressed. God sees the best in us, and past what everyone else looks at. God has no evaluation of you, but if a sovereign weight has to be transferred, you got to have the ability to be ready for it when. He wires it to you in your account.

That's why some of us right now, we have not got an unemployment check, we haven't got our stimulus check, we haven't got our income tax check, because we don't have anything in our spirits. It's empty in there! That means, after tonight, you will see why things are delayed, but it ain't denied. Tell somebody beside you, *it may be delayed, but it ain't denied.*

Because guess what: God is downloading truth and blessings in your spirit. This means that you're ready to receive it. If you're ready to put on your helmet, God will get ready to transfer something over. So now, I speak to sister Christy and say, "I'm about to get it and transfer it to you, but I can't transfer it to you until it first hits your spiritual account."

What do I mean by spiritual account? Your spiritual account is in your spirit. Remember, transfers in heaven cannot hit ugly accounts; it cannot hit earthly accounts, but it can only hit spiritual accounts. Tell somebody, *you got to put your helmet on and open your spiritual account.* I once told someone that they first have to believe. I told them this, but they got mad at me. I said, "You're not going to get anywhere if you don't believe. You've got to put this in your spirit, man!"

God will bless my spirit and, then, your spirit. He will reach sister Christy from His Spirit, and when she starts receiving it, then the baby can come! Then someone else can be blessed! Blessings are on the way, and this could be any time of any day. You hear me? Right now, I feel the Holy Ghost. This can be the hour that God speaks to your spirit. Whatever He's saying to you tonight, the Devil will not attack, because you've got heaven on you.

Glory to God! Whatever you want to come and happen right now, you already got your heaven on, so ask for this in Jesus' name. And when you get it, tell me what happened to you. When you receive from the Lord, when you start thinking in another dimension, let me know. This may sound crazy to people. But you start telling them, "I'm ready to preach. I'm ready to receive the blessings in my spirit first, because that's the way it works!"

Blessings Begin in the Spiritual Dimension

Because you have your helmet on, you start thinking in other dimensions. People might tell you, *you can't get that house*. Why? Because they do not have the same kind of thinking as you do. They're not on your same level, so it is impossible that you can't pay a bill, but God is ready to bless you with a house. Why do I say that? Because I've got my helmet on, and it means that the Devil cannot attack and hit what already belongs to me.

Tell somebody, *what belongs to me, is for me, and is duplicated for you*. Let the blessings continue for me and for you. Thank you, God! That means that what God is saying in your spirit—whatever is in your spirit—is on the way. If they still tell you that you can't have that house, it is because they are not thinking in the spirit, they are not operating in the spiritual dimensions, and they're just not seeing things the same way. They're going to think low, and you're going to think high. You've got the advantage, you've got the advice, and you've got the advance. When there's a wire transfer in the spiritual dimension, between heaven and your spirit, then you know that they don't really know anything about you.

Just get your new house. Don't worry about what they say. Just get your new car and drive up to your new property. We can walk up on anything we want to walk up. I can get ready to walk up on a midtown millionaire church—don't tell me what I can't have. Glory to God! God said whatever I ask I shall be given. This means that His Word shall not return back void.

Put this in your spirit first, and don't ignore the spiritual dimension. It's easy to believe only what you see. But God begins in places unseen. Put that job in your spirit first, and when you put that job in your spirit, then you take it. You take it, and when you take it from your spirit, into your mind, it will transfer from your mind into your life. Whatever you need God to work out for you, put it in your spirit.

Anything that you put in your spirit, may suddenly pop up in your mind. You know when people randomly pop up in your mind? You can be sitting at home and, sometimes, people pop up in your spirit. And the next thing you know, they either call you on your phone or they show up at your house. Who am I talking to right now? Just like putting that person in your spirit, put your finances in your spirit, too.

Glory to God, Hallelujah! God says that many of you are about to get a promotion. You have got to know that I'm talking to you, because I feel a promotion, and I feel it in your spirit. I don't care if you already have your business—I feel a promotion. Glory to God, I feel in my spirit that after this is over with, that promotion is coming.

Wait on the Lord

People can be so ugly, and they can have ugly spirits. We look at them, wondering how they could get that way. But sometimes, when people get hurt, in a way they don't deserve, they don't last long. Sometimes, I will wait upon the Lord, and pray I would be patient in these matters.

Psalm 27:14 (NIV) says, "Wait for the Lord; be strong and take heart and wait for the Lord." Are you waiting for the Lord to move? Or are you making your own timetable? Don't just wait for the Lord, but wait *patiently* for the Lord to act.

Job says to be patient and to wait upon the Lord. Some others will look at another and wonder why someone else got married and they're still not married. Why did someone else get promoted and I did not? I've come to tell you tonight to get ready for God to hit your spirit. He is about to get ready to show up, in this very minute you're in right now, I pray for God to sanctify you. God is getting ready to save you, and He is getting ready to deliver you.

He said this thing is getting ready to come to past, whatever it is that you're dealing with, and what you're going through, this, too, shall come to pass. Tell somebody, *it is ready to pass*. God is going to raise you to another level. Who am I talking to? Tonight, there is somebody here who is trusting God to get married. He's going to make you a beautiful wife in your spirit first. And you better listen and don't go too fast. Don't jump ahead because you're impatient. You get to be a beautiful wife in your spirit, and it's got to be in your spirit, because if ain't in your spirit, you must wait. Glory to God, you're going to be a beautiful wife. Beautiful is vain, trauma is deceitful, but the real beautiful in you is the part of you that is from above. You will become so irresistible that many people will approach you. And you'll have so many choices, and you'll have to say *not you, not you, not you*. But, I will choose you!

Hallelujah, thank you, God. Do you understand what I'm saying? You've got to have a new you. You've got to learn how to offer everything up to the Lord. Whatever people said you can't do, you can do. Some things inside of you are not consistent with what God told you to put in your spirit. So, diligently seek after the Lord. Meditate on the Lord, and ensure that He seals your mind and spiritually fills up your mind, too.

CHAPTER 7

LET GOD LET HIS LIGHT IN

Someone say, *Fill my mind, God. Fill my mind with peace.* Our minds needs to be filled. If you're listening clearly, you can sit at my table. If you're coming with a negative report, don't come with these negative thoughts, because they are contrary to His Spirit. Make yourself leave these thoughts outside on the doorsteps. These have no place in here. And if you're not sure you're thinking these thoughts, ask God to let His Light shine into your mind today and reveal them to you.

John 8:12 says that when Jesus spoke to the people, He said, "I am the light of the world. Whoever follows me will never walk in darkness, but will have the light of life." Hallelujah! Glory to God!

Let His Light Shine

God spoke to the darkness and said *let there be light!* And it wasn't out of fear. But some of us get fearful when we see darkness, instead of saying *let there be light*. Too many of us are in darkness, and sit in the darkness. We need to come out of darkness when we speak the Word out loud. We can't be afraid of the three-letter word, *let! Let* the Light of God shine! And *let* the Light of God in!

I John 1:5 (NIV) says, "God is light, and in Him is no darkness at all."

There are barriers in front of us, blockages that want to prevent something we want to happen from happening. Are you keeping God's Light out of your life? Are you choosing to stay in the darkness? God wants something to happen in your life. He wants to bring His Light in your life. What He did in creation, He will do in your life, too. He will make things beautiful, more beautiful than you ever imagined.

Glory to God! Hallelujah! Let there be light! And as He spoke to the darkness, He also speaks to the darkness of our minds. He will light up a light on the levels that we're in, so we can have more of the mind of Christ. Let this mind be in you, as was also in Christ Jesus.

God is Lifting You Up High

Just as God did with the creation of the world, He wants to do with us, His raw material.

God doesn't want you to walk to South Carolina; he wants you to fly to South Carolina. He doesn't want me to walk to Atlanta; he wants me to fly to Atlanta. Why? Because He wants me to be equal. Somebody better talk! What does equal mean, prophetess? Equal means equal.

To consider myself to be equal with God, that's how Christ's mind works. That's why Jesus said, "I and the Father are one." That's the mind He wants you to have, the same thinking that He has. He wants you to have the same thoughts that He has. It's not our way, but it's God's way. It's not my thoughts— it's God's thoughts. How He wants you to think is what mankind calls impossible. But God will reveal that it is possible.

God says He will reveal the impossible to you. It's not impossible that I purchase a church worth one million dollars. It's possible because of my faith, and because He no longer just wants to keep this blessing in the heavenly places. All of your blessings are in the heavenly places. If you now want it on earth, it starts in heaven. It's impossible for you, but it's possible for God. You've got to get in your spirit, and you've got to get it from heaven.

You're one thought away from the life God wants you to have. God gave us stuff, the life we have, and wants us to live out our dreams. He infused you with His Spirit. You are one thought away from your breakthrough, your next breakthrough, and the one after that. It will change your life completely. You're one foot away from God fulfilling your career. You're one foot away from the transformation of your life. Let God own your thinking. You got to put on the helmet: I want you to see it for yourself. And the only way that you're going to see it is to be in the Spirit. Once you got it in your spirit, you'll see the way God sees it.

CHAPTER 8

SALVATION—THE ULTIMATE DELIVERANCE

Today, the ultimate deliverance comes from the ultimate sacrifice of Jesus laying down His life for you and for me. In Romans 10:9 (NIV) it says, "that if you confess with your mouth the Lord Jesus and believe in your heart that God has raised Him from the dead, you will be saved." Hallelujah, glory to God!

Have you received this gift of salvation? It is available for anyone who confesses with their mouth the Lord Jesus and for anyone who believes in their heart God raised Jesus from the dead! Seize the moment, and don't let this pass by you. To be connected and one in Christ our Lord, we start with His salvation in our hearts.

Salvation in Our Hearts

People tell me that they're going to heaven. Baby, if your seat's already there, praise God. I want you all to understand this first. You're not always going to see an altar call for salvation. Salvation doesn't always take place when you come to an altar. Sometimes, I see people come to an altar, but salvation takes place in their hearts when they leave the altar, or when they're in their seats, or walking down the hallway. What invokes salvation is the Word of God, not the location.

When we receive salvation, it's supposed to start changing our minds, and changing our hearts. As you receive Jesus Christ as the only begotten Son, who was resurrected after His sacrifice for you on the cross of Calvary, this happens in our hearts. Whenever and wherever you were born again, you're already seated in heaven. The mission of the church is not to get to heaven, so let this mind be in you. Let your mind be of Christ as your heart receives salvation.

God is a Creator, and because of that, I am creative. God is righteous, so then I can be righteous. God is powerful, so now I have power. And if God can say no, then I can say no. God is the Deliverer, so we can be delivered in Christ Jesus. Let this mind be in you.

God Represents You

When Moses asked God what he should say when the Israelites asked who sent him, God told Moses to say, "I am that I Am." That's God's name, *I Am*, and not "I am that I Am". And when Moses said this to Pharaoh, he was essentially saying, *When you see me, you see God, and I can give you proof on that.*

You are the anointing, and the anointing is God, the Holy Spirit, and He lives inside of you. So, when God gives you thought processes, He didn't give them to you to frustrate you, but to reveal Himself to you, and represent you. And who better to represent you than the Almighty God? He is ready to represent you. Are you ready to represent Him?

Glory to God! God isn't trying to frustrate you, or bring you down. He comes to fulfill you. You just have to work, believe it, and put it in your spirit. Know that you have power, and this power is available to you to help you bring your thinking along, to pass it along to your generation and generations to come.

God is here to give you an advantage. How many of you like an advantage? He's here to give you an edge, place you a step above, and bring your mind into the heavenly places. God sees you exactly how He sees Christ—able and powerful—and that means that God can see you being powerful and above all because you are a joint heir of Christ and an heir of God.

My sisters and my brothers, you got to rise up above the earth, until the heaven clears and the Father is on His wings like an eagle. You've got to think above, you've got to live above your struggles, you've got to live above your pain, you've got to live above your crisis, you've got to live above your illness, your sickness, your disease, your trauma, temptations, and the tragedy you're going through. It's time to live above that, and think above it.

I'm bringing my sisters, my brothers, and everybody to the Word of God, to the Living God, to the power of God, and to the Lord Jesus Christ. And God, as I speak, is already around us, being our protection. God is surrounding us, brothers and sisters. Remember, our ultimate deliverance is salvation through Jesus Christ—Amen and amen!

CHAPTER 9

GOD DELIVERS US FROM EVIL AND DARKNESS

Put on the helmet of salvation ,so that your mind is protected. I pray your divine purpose and minds are protected by the supreme grace of God. Every foul spirit that is not like God shall not enter into the opportunity that He has given us right now. I declare that our lives are in your light, God, and that we shall come up into the heavenly places, and we shall get to have the blessings. In the name of Jesus, release the power unto our minds today, bringing into place everything that You say should be. We bind every spirit of hell, principality, evil power, and darkness working in our minds and on the Internet right now.

I bind it right now, and I cover our brothers and sisters right now. I cover our children and grandchildren right now. Whatever is in the dark places right now, God, you put Your Light on it, because you say in the Word, *let there be light*. We bind fear right now, Father, in the name of Jesus. I pray that you touch every one of them that is here, and that you shine light wherever darkness is right now. God, you shine light wherever sickness is right now. We bind the hand of the enemy right now, because you're here right now. We bind the hands of poverty right now, because you're the God who gives seed to the sower. and we're more than conquerors in Christ Jesus.

We thank You tonight for the Word that You have brought forth and that You have downloaded it into our spirits. God, You are in our spirits right now, so we ask that You send and transfer Your wealth into our accounts right now. Transfer the house that we have our desires set upon. Transfer the blessings into our spirits now, because we have the helmet of salvation on.

No Weapon Against Us Shall Prevail

No weapon that is formed against us shall hit us, because our helmets are on. The Word of God that we read tonight, is downloaded into our spirits now, and we're thinking right now. We're thinking and believing that You should shine Your Light on everyone that is called by You tonight, and wherever there is an enemy trying to hinder and put darkness there. I ask You, right now, to put Your Light on it and let this light shine, so that men and women shall see the glory that You put on them right now. And for the chosen tonight, God, put Your Light on them, and let them walk in the pathway You carve out for them to walk on. You said in Your Word that a good man's step is ordered by You. Order our steps tonight, God. Order our steps in the morning, God. Order our steps even starting next week, God, and download this in our spirits.

Even if we walk through the valley of the shadow of death, we fear no evil. You shall put down every evil door. Yes, we thank You right now, God, that Your Light is already working. That the Spirit is already working all things together for the good of them who love You. We love You tonight, God. We come with Your Word tonight and You said Your Word is like a two-edged sword. And God promises that we're already protected. You function with Your Word, with Your anointing, so we pray that You do it right now in the name of Jesus. Go into each and every one of our houses right now, God. I decree and I declare that this is a miracle night. Show Your glory, show Your anointing, and destroy anything that is dormant in our lives, and ready to wake up.

This, Too, Shall Pass

Lord, destroy any darkness in us right now. You've got the power, and You can do it, God. You gave us the power to speak, so I speak it, and I come with Your power. Let it hit the Universe, so that You turn everything around. And every time You turn things around, You keep on blessing us. God, in this season right now, during this coronavirus season, it is only temporary. The Word says this, too, shall pass, and God, You know the hour, You know the time, You know the days, You know the weeks, and You know the months. We know who we report to, and we still believe in the name of Jesus.

God, we thank for this word, and we thank You for downloading it in us. Let the Holy Ghost come, and let it come and lift up our spirits right now. We thank You right now, God, in the name of Jesus. We thank You that You are God. Let Your power fall, let Your glory fall, and let it fall on this house right now. Let Your anointing destroy the yoke that weighs us down, and let it destroy every foul spirit in the name of Jesus. God has already heard me. God, I believe You are already here. God, whoever is weak, I command that they got the strength to carry on. God, whoever is sick, I command that they're already healed.

And God, whoever is lonely, I declare that the lonely days are gone, and happy days are here. The joy of the Lord is our strength. Send strength here, God. Send strength to this house right now. Touch us right now, as we put our spiritual helmets on. We will do what Your Word says.

When we put our helmets on, it indicates what Your Word says and Your words shall not return back void. Your Word is eternal. Everything else will pass, but Your Word will remain forever. We give You glory tonight, and all glory belongs to You. I command, right now, that everyone who is here is shown Your glory, and shown Your power. Let them know that this was You tonight.

CHAPTER 10

A MIRACLE FOR YOU

In Jesus' name, I speak miracles of checks showing up by Wednesday, that employment will show up by Monday, and that God does a new thing in your lives. This is all about You, God. We put You on the line, as You say You'll go first, and You will take control. I give You glory, God. I give You glory right now for the miracles You shall perform in our house right now.

There are 30 people here now who will walk into Your calling and with Your anointing, God. You shall order their steps, You shall touch their hearts, and cover them by Your blood. Thank You for being our defense right now. You said if we abide in You, You would abide in us. We thank You, God.

You have been waiting on him or getting ready to return back to Him. God is going to touch the hearts of men and women today. It is your season to get His blessings, so be ready to receive them. Be strong, be not afraid, and don't you panic. Be not fearful, just be in God's power. And God says I'm going to do what I'm going to do. For the Lord, your God, is ahead of you, not behind you, and He shall do what He said He's going to do. He said He is a God who shall not lie, and neither shall He repent.

Listen to Delories Nunnery's story:

One day, I shared with Prophetess Merchele Robinson that my business was generating $3,000 - $4,000 each month. And, then, I started attending The Prophet House, in November of 2019. From that time on, I started seeing miracles manifesting in my business, Angel of Hope. And the prophetess challenged me to sow $300 into the ministry. So, I did. The very next week, my business started to make $15,000 - $16,000 every month! Hallelujah! I give all the glory to God! I had to hire three more drivers and buy two more vans. God opened up the doors and blessed me so abundantly, we bought a third van! One of my drivers ended up getting COVID-19 and needed to quarantine. Soon, God blessed me with a new driver. Although God doesn't need our money, when I sow my money unto God, I see blessings as a result.

A few months ago, I realized I did not pay for my business' insurance. So, I called the insurance company that same day. The insurance company told me that my business' insurance had already been paid for, and that I didn't need to worry about it! All glory to God!

Hallelujah! By the Spirit, it is already done. I want it in your spirit, and put it in your spirit. I see a miracle at 8 o'clock in the morning, and I see a miracle at 8 o'clock at night. We're getting ready to show up, glory to God!

Hallelujah! For some of you, I hear God saying that the miracle is in 72 hours. I hear God saying 72 hours. Glory to God for a 72-hour miracle. The Lord is saying *yes* to you. Your afflictions are just for a little while. And it's going to be all right. Hold your heads up! God said He will make the crooked ways straight. God is going to show you, God is going to enlighten your eyes, since you've been praying to the Lord. Get prepared. You have been holding your head down, but God says to keep it up! He's about to give you some more answers.

Minister Tracey Crawford's Story:

One day, God told Minister Tracey that life was about to change. That through me, blessings were going to flow. As we prayed together, Minister Tracey finally quit smoking and paid off all his bills. Glory to God! There were people working under Minister Tracey, at his job, who had been speaking lies about him. They purposely did this so the whole company would hear these lies, and they could set him up to be fired. But instead, God used me to prophesy to these people. Hallelujah. God intervened in Minister Tracey's life and the blessings flowed in his life.

Hallelujah! When this is over, God is going to send some of you to uncommon places—some places that you haven't been to—and you're going to travel there and cross over the waters. This will be a new dimension of God. Get ready for increase, and keep your hearts after God.

For a few of you, God is going to elevate you up. You're going to get the victory, and spiritually, you already got the victory. It was like you were down and God flipped it upside-down. You're getting ready to be above the situation, and God is turning it around for you. When God turns something around, it cannot be flipped back. Yes, the Lord is worthy, and the Lord is worthy to be praised.

Mirlene Georges' Story:

Even though business was very slow for Mirlene, she decided to sow a seed of $1,000 recently. And the very next day, her daughter called her with some good news. A check had arrived for her from a hotel she hadn't worked at in a while. Hallelujah! Then, Mirlene received a call from the company she worked for. They decided to give her a raise—glory to God! And not only did Mirlene get a raise, the company gave her backpay that was worth a whole month's salary. When I spoke into Mirlene's life, God broke through in her finances. Now, Mirlene believes in sowing her money into God, since it will return back a hundred fold.

Hallelujah! I see a blessing ready to hit some of your hands. Yes, I see some money getting ready to be wired to you. And I see God healing some of you. By His stripes, you are already healed. Just go and receive it—you're already healed!

CHAPTER 11

GIVING BACK TO THE LORD

Always be ready to take out your tithes and offerings to sow into the ministry of the Lord. Whether it is $7 or $17, listen to God speaking to your heart and sow into the Word of God. It says in 2 Corinthians 9:7 (NIV), "Each of you should give what you have decided in your heart to give, not reluctantly or under compulsion, for God loves a cheerful giver."

Whichever number God puts on your heart, that's what you do. Put on the helmet of salvation and sow this seed as your miracle. God knows the heart of man, and He is challenging you today. Those who God is speaking to, listen carefully. He wants to sow blessings into your life today.

Tithes and Offerings—What's the Difference?

In Hebrew, *tithe,* means *tenth.* Tithing 10 percent of our income is the standard. And this is meant to protect you, not punish you. If you don't give 10 percent, nobody's going to kill you or harm you. But by *not* tithing, we are endangering our lives, and not protecting them. It's time to honor this standard set by God. He truly knows what is best for us.

If you've got an offering, this is on top of your tithing—Hallelujah! Some of you have an abundance which you can give from, and others only have a little. This makes no difference to Him. Let's show God what kind of managers of His money we are. Let's not be selfish. Anyone who is being selfish or has a spirit of selfishness is living in brokenness, and in poverty.

Anyone who is selfish has a tight-fisted hand. If you have a tight-fisted hand, you won't give, nor can you be open to receiving any blessings. When you give someone a gift, and they're tight-fisted, they won't get to receive your gift. In the same way, we need to keep our hands open. We need to learn to give freely and receive freely from the Lord. Hallelujah!

Some of you might be saying, "Prophetess, I've never sowed before, but you touch my heart today. I'm going to do this because I've been in the battle of the mind for too long. I've had a double mind, and I'm ready to put on the helmet of salvation and sow into God's blessings for me."

Amen! When you do this, God is going to protect your mind. Yes, He is going to protect your mind. He's going to bring what He says to pass. God doesn't need our money. He's a spiritual God, and He's already got everything in His hands! It's man who is the creator of money. It doesn't make any sense to try and hold onto something that doesn't belong to you in the first place. And we're never going to get to keep anything, including money, anyways!

Invest in the Lord, and He will Invest in You

Giving our money to the Lord shows our heart. It shows we're not greedy, selfish, or in love with money. It's when we give our money to the works of God that the wealth can be wisely distributed. Glory to God!

If you want God to invest in you, invest in Him. Invest in His virtue. Invest in His increase. If we're not consistently investing in Him, why should He invest in someone who doesn't make a return to Him? Even in today's world, many people are driven by money. And no investor is going to invest in someone who is a worthless investment. No one is going to keep giving when they're not getting anything in return.

My burden of proof is to assure and show God that I am an inveritable investment to make. I prove this to Him by investing out of the increase and harvest I receive in my life. Or the little that I do have, I give in faith in Him. Give as God has prospered you! Give as God has increased you!

Let me say a final prayer for you:

> *Father, we thank you for the ones who gave tonight, and even the ones who didn't have anything to give. Touch our hearts, and release miracles to each and every one of us today. We pray over this offering, that You do an overflow, that You show us a miracle, and that You rebuke every devourer for our sake. We thank You right now. We pray that You release Your miracles, release Your anointing, and bless these seeds a hundred fold, in Jesus' name, I pray.*

www.ingramcontent.com/pod-product-compliance
Lightning Source LLC
LaVergne TN
LVHW020440080526
838202LV00055B/5281